SPELLING PRACTICE SHEETS

For use with
Traditional Spelling Book Two

Cheryl Lowe

MEMORIA PRESS
www.MemoriaPress.com

SPELLING PRACTICE SHEETS
For use with *Traditional Spelling Book Two*

Cheryl Lowe

ISBN 978-1-61538-984-1

Cover illustration by Hannah Thibaudeau

CONTENTS

Lesson 1: CVC & CVCC words w/final consonant teams 4
Lesson 2: CVC & CVCC words w/final consonant blends 5
Lesson 3: Long ā (silent **e**; vowel teams **ay, ai**) 6
Lesson 4: Long ē (vowel teams **ee, ea**) 7
Lesson 5: Long ī (silent **e**; **i** before two consonants; vowel team **igh**) 8
Lesson 6: Long ō (silent **e**; **o** before two consonants; vowel teams **oe, oa, ow**) 9
Lesson 7: Long ū (silent **e**; vowel teams **ue, ui**) 10
Lesson 8: Vowel teams for **/o͞o/** (**ew, oo, ou**) 11
Lesson 9: Hard and soft **c** and **g** 12
Lesson 10: **h**-teams (**ch, sh, th, wh**) 13
Lesson 11: Initial consonant blends (**s, r, l**) 14
Lesson 12: Three more consonant teams (**qu, dge, tch**) 15
Lesson 13: Three-letter consonant blends 16
Lesson 14: Three sounds of **y** (/y/, /ī/, /ē/) 17
Lesson 15: Three sounds of **ey** (/ā/, /ē/) 18
Lesson 16: Vowel teams for **/oi/** (**oi, oy**) and **/ou/** (**ou, ow**) 19
Lesson 17: Three more spellings of /ŭ/ (**oo, ou, o**) 20
Lesson 18: Words ending in /əl/ spelled **le** (**le** syllables) 21
Lesson 19: Words ending in /əl/ spelled **el** 22
Lesson 20: **r**-controlled vowel **/âr/** (**air, are, ear**) 23
Lesson 21: **r**-controlled vowel **/ûr/** (**er, ir, ur**) 24
Lesson 22: Consonant teams with silent letters (**mb, kn, wr**) 25
Lesson 23: Contractions 26
Lesson 24: Plurals that add **-es** 27
Lesson 25: Irregular plurals 28
Lesson 26: Double Rule (1-1-1 words) 29
Lesson 27: Drop Rule (silent **e**) 30
Lesson 28: Change Rule (**y** to **i**) 31
Lesson 29: Compounds words; words accented on last syllable 32
Lesson 30: Prefixes and suffixes 33
Lesson 31: Two more vowel teams for /ē/ (**ei, ie**); "**i** before **e** except after **c**" rule, part 1 34
Lesson 32: Two more vowel teams for /ā/ (**ei, eigh**); "**i** before **e** except after **c**" rule, part 2 35
Lesson 33: Homophones 36
Lesson 34: Vowel teams for /ô/ (**aw, au, al/all**) 38

**These Practice Sheets may be reproduced for a single student within your own home.*

LESSON 1

Name:

1. sing
2. tell
3. pass
4. thanks
5. king
6. pack
7. ink
8. pick
9. junk
10. lock
11. long
12. cuff
13. jazz
14. **does**
15. **been**

LESSON 2

Name:

1. end
2. wind
3. camp
4. elf
5. melt
6. help
7. next
8. kept
9. lift
10. just
11. sent
12. silk
13. past
14. **said**
15. **who**

LESSON 3

Name:

1. today
2. mail
3. late
4. awake
5. daisy
6. gave
7. railway
8. ate
9. main
10. raise
11. paid
12. paint
13. safe
14. pray
15. **says**

LESSON 4

Name:

1. dear
2. street
3. teach
4. seen
5. speak
6. real
7. greeting
8. sweet
9. sea
10. clean
11. queen
12. bee
13. please
14. **even**
15. **people**

LESSON 5

Name:

1. size
2. wild
3. pint
4. white
5. high
6. tide
7. right
8. mind
9. night
10. fire
11. child
12. light
13. **good-bye**
14. **buy**
15. **eye**

LESSON 6

Name:

1. nose
2. follow
3. cold
4. throat
5. colt
6. coach
7. shadow
8. toe
9. toast
10. doe
11. yellow
12. joke
13. bowl
14. goes
15. broke

LESSON 7

Name:

1. fuse
2. cure
3. bruise
4. Sue
5. rudely
6. cube
7. mute
8. costume
9. mule
10. juicy
11. glue
12. Tuesday
13. **sure**
14. **Ruth**
15. **truth**

LESSON 8

Name: ____________________

1. threw
2. chew
3. root
4. wound
5. soothe
6. strew
7. tooth
8. pew
9. stew
10. stool
11. loose
12. youth
13. troop
14. flew
15. moon

LESSON 9

Name: ____________________

1. circle
2. giant
3. peace
4. dance
5. circus
6. wagon
7. center
8. given
9. change
10. dingy
11. rage
12. cellar
13. **hunger**
14. **once**
15. **begin**

LESSON 10

Name:

1. them
2. shell
3. brush
4. church
5. think
6. push
7. much
8. path
9. with
10. these
11. check
12. which
13. fresh
14. lunch
15. while

LESSON 11

Name:

1. smile
2. skip
3. brick
4. frost
5. prize
6. plant
7. drive
8. glad
9. club
10. snake
11. score
12. stand
13. truck
14. crack
15. blend

LESSON 12

Name:

1. catch
2. itch
3. quack
4. edge
5. quick
6. pitch
7. quit
8. pledge
9. badge
10. bridge
11. quiz
12. quite
13. dodge
14. fudge
15. match

LESSON 13

Name:

1. shrimp
2. scrap
3. squid
4. shrug
5. strap
6. split
7. spring
8. shrink
9. thrill
10. strong
11. scratch
12. square
13. should
14. would
15. could

LESSON 14

Name:

1. fly
2. ninety
3. pretty
4. easy
5. angry
6. family
7. beyond
8. really
9. shy
10. try
11. yard
12. sly
13. forty
14. carry
15. any

LESSON 15

Name:

1. hockey
2. they
3. key
4. alley
5. donkey
6. journey
7. hey
8. valley
9. monkey
10. honey
11. chimney
12. prey
13. obey
14. turkey
15. volley

LESSON 16

Name:

1. voice
2. town
3. joint
4. pout
5. avoid
6. noisy
7. bounce
8. blouse
9. plow
10. clown
11. south
12. powder
13. enjoy
14. annoy
15. crown

LESSON 17

Name:

1. flood
2. double
3. oven
4. touch
5. other
6. mother
7. young
8. come
9. couple
10. blood
11. won
12. son
13. brother
14. cousin
15. trouble

LESSON 18

Name:

1. cradle
2. stable
3. thimble
4. swaddle
5. bugle
6. middle
7. bubble
8. bottle
9. single
10. eagle
11. needle
12. noble
13. gentle
14. muscle
15. title

LESSON 19

Name:

1. novel
2. chapel
3. travel
4. barrel
5. angel
6. nickel
7. tunnel
8. camel
9. jewel
10. shovel
11. label
12. kernel
13. bushel
14. channel
15. flannel

LESSON 20

Name:

1. tear
2. lair
3. fair
4. wear
5. fairy
6. rare
7. pair
8. glare
9. pear
10. stair
11. snare
12. scare
13. bear
14. dare
15. share

LESSON 21

Name:

1. shirt
2. birth
3. sturdy
4. burst
5. blurry
6. nursery
7. perch
8. purple
9. verb
10. purse
11. skirt
12. thirsty
13. squirrel
14. germ
15. urge

LESSON 22

Name:

1. knew
2. limb
3. knead
4. wren
5. knot
6. wreath
7. knob
8. wrote
9. knock
10. wrap
11. climber
12. comb
13. knight
14. wrench
15. crumb

LESSON 23

Name:

1. I'd
2. wouldn't
3. you've
4. they've
5. what's
6. they'll
7. who's
8. couldn't
9. they're
10. weren't
11. she'll
12. he'll
13. hadn't
14. shouldn't
15. she's

LESSON 24

Name:

1. bunches
2. halves
3. taxes
4. selves
5. dishes
6. wolves
7. inches
8. scarves
9. lives
10. branches
11. leaves
12. loaves
13. peaches
14. calves
15. knives

LESSON 25

Name:

1. oxen
2. children
3. heroes
4. men
5. potatoes
6. women
7. tomatoes
8. mice
9. sheep
10. geese
11. scissors
12. teeth
13. trout
14. feet
15. deer

LESSON 26

Name:

1. boxing
2. enjoyed
3. thinnest
4. player
5. mopped
6. slowest
7. quizzing
8. fittest
9. snowing
10. batter
11. tripped
12. mixed
13. flipping
14. mowed
15. jogger

LESSON 27

Name:

1. lonely
2. smiling
3. liking
4. bravest
5. likeness
6. hopeless
7. skating
8. safety
9. shameful
10. moving
11. icing
12. homeless
13. likely
14. grading
15. useful

LESSON 28

Name:

1. staying
2. stayed
3. carrying
4. carried
5. studying
6. studied
7. playing
8. played
9. crying
10. cried
11. prettier
12. happily
13. hurrying
14. hurried
15. flying

LESSON 29

Name:

1. beneath
2. firefly
3. ahead
4. someone
5. asleep
6. keyboard
7. against
8. airport
9. notebook
10. afraid
11. homework
12. before
13. baseball
14. besides
15. nowhere

LESSON 30

Name:

1. useless
2. friendship
3. illness
4. expect
5. unable
6. unknown
7. quickly
8. enjoyment
9. except
10. careful
11. falsehood
12. freedom
13. incline
14. increase
15. disgrace

LESSON 31

Name:

1. believe
2. niece
3. receive
4. grieve
5. deceive
6. shield
7. field
8. conceited
9. yield
10. ceiling
11. shriek
12. brief
13. chief
14. piece
15. thief

LESSON 32

Name:

1. reindeer
2. sleigh
3. their
4. heir
5. freight
6. neighbor
7. veil
8. weigh
9. eight
10. vein
11. seize
12. neither
13. either
14. weird
15. protein

LESSON 33

Name:

1. dear
2. deer
3. blue
4. blew
5. sail
6. sale
7. would
8. wood
9. our
10. hour
11. ate
12. eight
13. hole
14. whole

15. hear

16. here

17. to

18. too

19. two

20. sew

21. sow

22. so

LESSON 34

Name:

1. halluway
2. small
3. already
4. almost
5. stall
6. false
7. haul
8. hawk
9. author
10. straw
11. because
12. yawn
13. always
14. softball
15. claw